Scientific Wire Company have supplied Maria Kerr with many types of wire for many years.

Established 44 years and one of the worlds leading producers and distributors of wire to the craft, textile and electronic sectors.

We are honoured to have cooperated with Maria and Charles Kerr in the production of this book that we hope will help readers in Malta and around the world to master the craft.

For Scientific Wire Company

Raphael Kodesh

Scientific Wire Company
18 Raven Road
London E18 1HW
Tel: 0044 208 505 0002
Fax: 0044 208 559 1114

wire@enterprise.net
www.wires.co.uk

GANUTELL

The Maltese Art
Of Making
Artistic Flowers

Maria Kerr

Edited by
Charles Kerr

GANUTELL

The Maltese Art of Making Artistic Flowers

Written by Maria Kerr and edited by Charles Kerr
Designed by Roderick Cohen

First Published in 2004 by The Scientific Wire Company
18,Raven Road, London, E18 1HW, England

ISBN 0-9549-3990-5

Printed in China

For our children,

their spouses and

our grandchildren

TABLE OF CONTENTS

FOREWORD

Notwithstanding the fact that Ganutell can trace its lineage to a number of European countries, the way it eventually evolved has definitely made it Maltese. Prior to the last decade of the twentieth century, Ganutell was on the verge of being another forgotten craft and few were those who knew what the word meant let alone create beautiful works of art. This sad state of affairs could be attributed to lack of interest, which in turn could have been due to ignorance of the techniques and qualities of Ganutell. Like most other craft that have their beginnings shrouded in the mists of time, the techniques have been passed on from generation to generation with little or no documentation.

In the beginning of the 1990's, the ailing craft was well on its way to recovery, and very soon Ganutell was taken up by a considerable number of people. This interest unfortunately had a negative aspect. The basic technique of this craft being relatively simple together with the large demand for lessons, made it very convenient for students to become "teachers" overnight. The lack of expertise when it comes to design, combination of colours and use of the proper materials; the lack of experience to artistically mount the project, coupled with the lack of books on the subject only helped to produce mediocre results.

A number of books are now available, these however are for local consumption, and are rather limited in the material and techniques they project. It was the lack of proper documentation of the various ganutell techniques and a genuine desire to teach and raise standards that led to the publication of this book. It was decided to present this book in English as it is felt that this art has the potential to appeal to all those who admire beauty irrespective of nationality.

We hope that this book will be found of interest and also help those who would like to improve their work.

Charles Kerr
Malta

INTRODUCTION

Arts and crafts in some form or another have existed since the dawn of man but constant advances reached a peak by the eighteenth century when lifestyle, costume and activities forced the decorative arts to develop their numerous forms, techniques and materials to satisfy the needs of flamboyant personal adornment, elaborate ceremonies and extravagant decoration of the churches and palaces of powerful royalty and rich nobility.

Vestments, banners, church and palace furnishings were intricately decorated by hand. Fabrics were expertly quilted, pleated, decorated in intricate techniques including lacework and embroidery in gold, silver and other metal thread, incorporating numerous types of ribbons, beads or margarites, glass tubes or pivettes, chenille, sequins and bouillon or spiral wires otherwise known in Malta as ganutell, and other available materials.

Personal adornment for women, depending on prevailing fashion, often included the addition of artificial sprays and flowers made of combinations of the various materials just mentioned, but especially of fabric or batiste and fortified with plain or spiral decorative gold and silver wire. Flowers were also handmade in fabric or wire forms for decorating altars, statues, niches, relics and innumerable other possible objects in churches and palaces with garlands, rosettes and mounts.

The demand for decorative crafts was satisfied mainly by monasteries and convents where the nuns and friars kept themselves profitably busy. The general terms of monastery craft or cloistercraft are used to refer to all sorts of different crafts that could be undertaken in convents, including wirework, shellcraft, embroidery, beadwork, ganutell, leathercraft, poker, lace, quilling, painting, gilding and many others. But monasteries were by no means the only sources for such work because numerous individuals and families worked in the home or workshops scattered in all towns and villages. Especially in the nineteenth and early twentieth centuries various craft schools were opened which included embroidery and artificial flower making for girls. Whether the crafts are undertaken in monasteries or not we still apply the term monastery craft to these various techniques, especially when they involve holy or devotional objects and subjects. These same crafts also produced work to satisfy mundane and non-religious demands. In various exhibitions held in England in the nineteenth and twentieth centuries to promote work from Empire countries, Malta was always represented with samples of all its industries including artificial and ganutell flowers.

Numerous references are met with in Maltese eighteenth and nineteenth century history when mounts of artificial flowers were presented to personalities during important ceremonies, especially grand masters making official visits to towns and villages or when officially installed at Birgu and Mdina. The same was done when bishops and parish priests officially assumed office or princes and important nobles visited Malta. Grand masters also sent similar symbolic forms to monarchs in other countries. Wealthy families often exchanged shades of artificial flowers, including ganutell, as wedding presents.

The Maltese term ganutell is a corruption of the Italian *cannotiglio* or Spanish *Canotilla* which is strictly the name of spiral, expandable wire or bouillon, used in various types of decorative embroidery, but in Malta it is a term adopted to stand not only for work involving this wire, but also to a mixture of other techniques which may or may not include any "ganutell" expandable wire, but even only wire, thread, beads, pearls, chenille and sequins. We can say that traditional Maltese ganutell style has a character of its own, involving all of these techniques, with very intricate and delicate work, as may be seen in the hundreds of free standing beautiful mounts which decorate the altars of our churches during festive occasions.

After the revival of this craft in the later years of the twentieth century some ganutell workers adopted styles which were not particularly favored by older generations mainly because many now aim mostly at producing hand sprays, tiaras, brooches and other personal effects for weddings, children's first Communion, Confirmation and other special occasions when these flowers have to be handled, carried and otherwise ill-treated, so that here the technique avoids the use of delicate expandable wire for the easier, quicker and more durable styles.

As a craft ganutell is traditional but the modern ganutell is not always the traditional in style. Like all the arts and crafts, traditional ganutell work is usually more time consuming, costly, elaborate and therefore definitely always beautiful, decorative and where appropriate worthy of being mounted in a glass dome for the permanent admiration of the different materials and techniques which go to make it, but the style adopted in some modern work should not be called traditional ganutell, but described as modern style ganutell.

This book describes numerous delicately executed techniques used in this craft and it should remain as a reliable guide to ensure the survival of the traditional style of Maltese ganutell.

Guido Lanfranco
Malta

GANUTELL
The Maltese Art of Making Artistic Flowers

Ganutell is the name of a Maltese craft that has been practised for centuries. Using various wires and thread, the artist can create a vast number of beautiful flowers having plain or decorated petals. The technique is simple enough but perfection comes only with practice.

Tools

Except for a spindle, no special tools are required. All the necessary tools can be easily obtained from hardware stores.

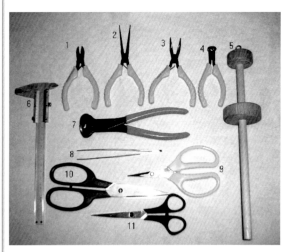

1 Side Cutter
2 Long Nose Pliers
3 Bent Nose Pliers
4 Cutter
5 Spindle
6 Calipers
7 Heavy Duty Cutter
8 Tweezers
9-10-11 Scissors

With the exception of the Heavy Duty Cutter, we suggest that you procure the type of tools normally used by electronic engineers, as these tools are not so bulky.

The spindle is normally found in hobby shops. It consists of a 30 cm dowel connecting two wooden discs with a hook on top. It is important that the spindle is well balanced and heavy enough to give a good spin. Initially you will need at least three spindles.

Materials

Rayon Floss

This type of thread is composed of six strands. Normally sold in skeins, it is available in over a hundred colours. The exceptional brilliance of the thread makes Rayon Floss an excellent medium.

Thickness	Type	Use
❋ 0.2mm	Tinned copper Coloured copper	Mounting Thread preparation
❋ 0.25mm	Silver / gold plated copper Corrugated also known as "Farfalla"	Thread preparation Decorating petals
❋ 0.4mm	Silver / gold plated copper	Stems
❋ 0.5mm	Tinned copper Silver/gold plated copper	Stems Stems for flowers worked with wire
❋ 0.6mm	Silver/gold plated copper Coloured copper	Stems for one layered flowers
❋ 1-1.5mm	Galvanised wire	Anima.
❋ Ganutell	Also known as bouillon and elastic wire	Stamens, decoration and flowers
❋ Molla	Spiral Wire	Flowers and leaves
❋ Beads	Gold, silver and glass beads	Stamens, decorate leaves and flowers

Petals are made of thread and wire spun together. This will be referred to as "prepared thread".

Thread

1. Having chosen the colour, uncoil the skein

2. Hold one end of the thread between forefinger and thumb of left hand and gently tease out one of the six strands. (fig 1). If during this operation the strand gets stuck, DO NOT use force   but stop pulling and give a gentle tug at the "tail end". When all the strands are teased out, pair them up, and tie the three pairs end to end

3. Attach one pair of strands and 0.2mm silver, gold or coloured wire to the hook on the top of the spindle (fig 2). Mete out about 50cm. of thread and wire and while sitting down holding the thread and wire in the left hand, push the lower part of the spindle against your thigh in an outward motion (fig. 3). This movement will cause the spindle to  spin. When the spindle stops spinning, repeat until  strands and wire are evenly entwined. Wind the thread between the discs, mete out another length and once again passing the thread through the hook (fig 4), repeat the process. Repeat until all strands have been used.

Wire

Gold plated, Silver plated, Coloured or Tinned copper wire of various thickness (see Table) is normally bought on reels. To obtain the best result, the piece of wire you intend to use for the stem should be as straight as possible.

Unwind about half a metre of wire from reel. Place reel on side on a flat surface and holding it down with left hand, stretch length using pliers. When taut, cut into required lengths

3 The Basic Petal

The basic petal is used for leaves and for making a considerable number of different flowers. Petals may be plain or decorated. Plain petals are used to make gladiolus, freesia, lilium, hyacinth and also one or two layered flowers while fancy flowers are made from the decorated petals. Petals may be decorated using, glass beads, rice beads, ganutell, corrugated wire and also spiral wire. Keep to the basic principles, then let your imagination run wild!

You will find that the technique is simple and it does not take a novice long to master it. Perfection, however, will not be achieved without patience and lots of practice.

MATERIALS

* *Stretched piece Copper Wire (0.5mm) approx 6cm long.*
* *Prepared Thread.*

TOOLS

Scissors.
Tweezers.
Calipers.

METHOD

1. Cut a piece of copper wire (0.5mm) 6cm long for stem of petal.
2. Hold stem about 1.5cm from one end in left hand between forefinger and thumb.
3. Place prepared thread between forefinger and thumb and with thread lying against stem, work five rounds. (fig 3.1)

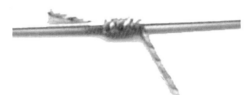

fig 3.1: work five rounds on stem

4. With stem in left hand, turn stem anti clockwise, take forward prepared thread and work one round next to starting point, trapping end of prepared thread. Trim protruding thread. (fig 3.2)

fig 3.2: work one round next to starting point

5. Turn stem again anticlockwise, take forward thread and work another round next to the first round.

6. Using this process, continue working till the desired measurement is obtained.

7. When the desired length is reached, finish off by working two rounds at the base of the petal. (fig.3.3) Trim thread.

fig 3.3: work two rounds at the base of petal

8. To complete petal, measure off 4mm from top of petal and cut off remaining length. Using tweezers bend top part of stem backward forming a hook.

When working on the basic petal you must make sure that the rounds are lying tightly against each other and that they do not overlap.

Basic Petal

Leaves

Leaves play a very important part in any arrangement no matter how small. They not only enhance your project but also decorate and complete your floral mount.

COLOUR

Leaves can be worked in all shades of green, various shades of brown and in particular cases also in gold or silver. The size of the leaf varies depending on the size of the flower.

METHOD

A leaf is worked in the same way as a basic petal, the only difference being in the number of rounds made at the start. As a general rule, leaves require a minimum of nine rounds.

SHAPE

The number of "starting" rounds made will determine the shape of the leaf. Increasing the number of rounds will give you an elongated leaf.

TYPES

This section covers three different types of leaves: The leaf, the long leaf, and spiral wire leaf. The latter will be discussed in Section 30, which is devoted to working with spiral wires.

Group of Three Leaves

MATERIALS

❀ *Green prepared thread.*
❀ *Stretched piece Copper Wire (0.5mm) approx 6cm long*
❀ *Copper wire (0.2mm)*
❀ *Floral tape*

TOOLS

Scissors
Tweezers
Calipers

1ST METHOD

1. Using green prepared thread and using the same method as the basic petal, make three leaves 1.9cm long, starting with nine rounds and finishing off with ten rounds instead of the two described in the basic petal.

2. Cover stems with floral tape, starting on fifth round on stem. (See Tips on Floral Tape at the end of this section).

3. Place two leaves over each other in such a way that the top leaf reaches mid-way up the bottom leaf.

4. Starting about 1cm away from the base of the leaf bind stems together by winding three or four rounds of copper wire (0.2mm) around the stems.

5. Cover the rounds of copper wire with floral tape.

6. Repeat process, placing the third leaf on top. Cover stems with floral tape.

7. Use tweezers to shape leaves

1. Using the same technique and measurements as shown in the first method make 3 leaves and cover stems with floral tape.

2. Place leaves next to each other with the middle leaf slightly higher than the other two.

3. Starting about 1cm away from the base of the lowest leaf bind stems together by winding three or four rounds of copper wire (0.2mm) around the stems.

4. Complete process by covering stems with floral tape and shaping leaves.

Group of Five Leaves

1. Using the same technique used for the basic leaf, make 5 leaves one of which measures 1.8cm and the remaining four each measuring 2.0cm.

2. Place leaf measuring 1.8cm in the middle with a larger leaf on either side in such a way that the central leaf is 1 cm higher than the other two.

3. Bind stems and cover with floral tape.

4. Place the remaining leaves one on either side, maintaining the same distance between leaves.

METHOD

5. Bind stems and cover with floral tape. Finish off by shaping leaves.

1. Make 5 leaves one measuring 2.0cm and the remaining four 1.8cm each.
2. Place a small leaf on top and another under the larger leaf.
3. Using copper wire (0.2mm) bind stems by winding two or three rounds.
4. Place one of the two remaining leaves in front of the bound leaves and the other one at the back.
5. Securely bind the stems together.
6. Cover with floral tape.
7. Hold work and using tweezers, twist first and second
8. leaf to the right and last two leaves to the left

> **Tip.**
> *When using floral tape to cover stems, cut tape in half, place tape beneath stem holding both between forefinger and thumb. Twirl flower between fingers and at the same time stretch tape at an angle to the flower.*

The long leaf

MATERIALS

* *Green thread (one strand)*
* *Cardboard*
* *PVA Glue*
* *Green wire (0.5mm)*
* *Floral tape*

TOOLS

Paint brush
Scissors
Tweezers

1ST METHOD

1. Fold cardboard down the centre and draw outline of half the leaf on one side.
2. Carefully cut along outline. Place pattern on another piece of cardboard and cut out another leaf.
3. Cut one piece of green wire (0.5mm) equal to the length of the leaf + 5cm for stem.
4. Apply glue to one side of leaf and place wire down the

centre in such a way that it protrudes about 3 mm from the tip of the leaf. Place thread next to wire starting from the middle of the leaf and going out at the tip of the leaf. Place thread next to wire starting from the middle of the leaf and going out at the tip. Cover with other leaf, press and allow to dry.

5. Apply glue, covering about 1cm from top of leaf. Work two rounds with the protruding thread around protruding wire and using tweezers bend wire towards back forming a hook.

6. Wind the thread around leaf laying the strands next to each other making sure that hook is covered. Continue applying glue and winding the thread until cardboard leaf is totally covered.

7. Tie a knot at the base of the leaf; trim thread and complete process by covering stem with floral tape.

1. Work leaf as described in the 1st Method but instead of trimming thread next to the end knot, allow a length of about 30 cm.

2. With the aid of a sewing needle, starting on the front side and as close as possible to the base, work two small stitches in the centre of the leaf.

3. Work one long stitch followed by two small stitches as near as possible to the tip of the leaf.

4. Return to the base of leaf and complete process by tying a knot at the base of the leaf and covering stem with floral tape

1. Cut out two leaves as described in the first method and a piece of copper wire (0.5mm) measuring double the total length of the leaf + 10 cms.

2. Apply glue to one side of leaf. Fold wire in two, ensuring that the wires are slightly apart and place on leaf. Place end of thread about a quarter of the way down the leaf and going out of the tip.

3. Cover with other leaf, press and allow to dry.

4. Slit leaf down the middle starting from the bottom right up to 1 cm from top.

5. Apply glue to the top 1cm of leaf, back and front, and wind the thread around the leaf laying the strands next to each other. Continue until slit is reached.

6. When slit is reached, slide thread through slit, cover back, bring thread to front, then through slit and to the back. Continue this "figure of eight" pattern of working until about 1cm from base. Apply glue and wind thread around the leaf until the end is reached.

7. Finish off by tying a knot at the base of the leaf and covering the two wires which form the stem with floral tape.

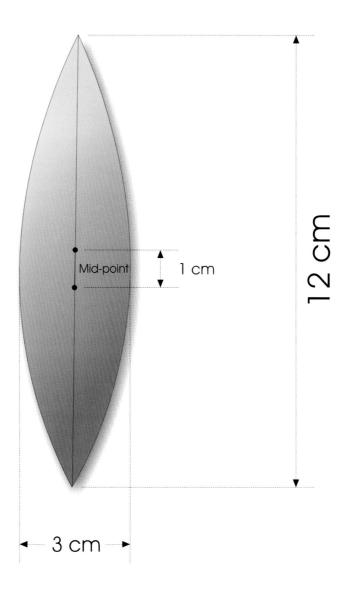

Mid-point

1 cm

12 cm

3 cm

The Long Leaf

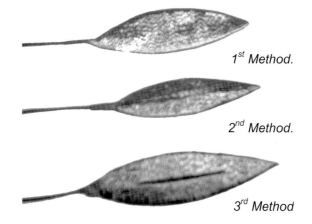

1st Method.

2nd Method.

3rd Method

Stamens

In nature stamens are an important part of the flower, in Ganutell stamens help to further decorate the flower, making it more attractive and eye catching.

Stamens may be simple or complicated, depending on the flower and on your imagination. Rhine stones, glass beads, gold and silver beads, pearls, ganutell and also chenille may be used to make stamens. Ready made stamens in various sizes and colours are also available, discerning artists however prefer to make their own as this would ensure that the stamens compliment the flower.

Knowledge of the basic beading technique helps when using beads to make stamens and a brief description is given in this section. Instructions on making chenille, which is mostly used when working gerberas, passionflowers and others is given in the chenille section.

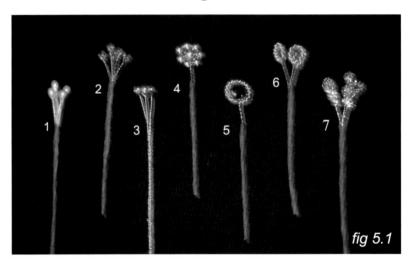

fig 5.1

The figure shows a number of stamens ranging from simple to slightly more complicated. This is far from being the complete range, using the same materials, and techniques do not be afraid to experiment.

Stamen 1 consists of a bunch of 5 ready-made stamens, these may be bought from most hobby shops.

Stamen 2 is made of five coloured beads, beaded individually and then bound in a bunch.

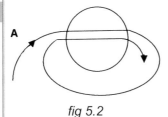

fig 5.2

Cut a piece of silver or gold wire 0.25mm, 11 cms. long. Place bead in the middle of the wire, insert one end through the bead once again and tighten. Bring ends together and holding them with a long nose plier, twist bead until wire is neatly twisted, forming the stem.

Stamen 3 is composed of three silver pearls individually beaded and bound. To bead the silver pearls use the same method described for Stamen 2.

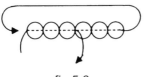

fig 5.3

Stamen 4 is a cluster of silver pearls with a gold pearl in the centre.

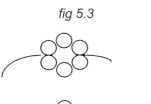

Cut a piece of silver or gold wire 0.25mm, 25cms long. Place six silver pearls on the centre of your wire. Run one end of the wire through 3 of those pearls. (fig 5.3) Gently pull ends to form a circle.

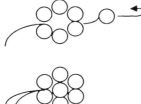

fig 5.4

Place a gold pearl on the wire that went through the three pearls. Bring the pearl down so that it rests in the center of the circle.

Twist the two wires together. Keep twisting till the wires forming the stem are neatly twisted.

Stamen 5 is simple yet attractive and consists of a rhine stone trimmed with ganutell.

Cut two pieces of wire 0.25mm, 10 cms long. Thread the two pieces through the cross at the back of the rhinestone, place stone in the centre, bend and twist wires making sure that the stem (twisted wires) is in the centre of the stone. Cut a piece of ganutell equal to the circumference of the stone and thread a piece of wire through it. Pull ends to form a circle and thread wire through back of stone, tighten and twist wire round stem. Press ganutell ring over the rhinestone.

Stamen 6 is made of three individual ganutell loops bound together,

METHOD

Thread a piece of ganutell about 1cm long and place in the middle of a piece of gold or silver wire 0.25mm, about 10cm long. Using technique described under Stamens 2, tighten ends to form a loop and twist stems. Loop the required number of stamens and using 0.2mm wire, bind together.

Stamen 7 consists of three separate pieces of twisted ganutell, bound together.

METHOD

Cut a piece of gold or silver wire 0.25mm, about 8 cm long and thread it through a piece of ganutell 2.5 cm long so that the ganutell is in the middle of the wire. Bring ends of wire together and inverting the spindle, pass the hook through the middle of the ganutell. Using a long nose pliers hold ends and turn spindle, twisting stem and ganutell. Work the required number and twist or bind together.

Detail from Mount Shades of Lilac.

In Nature the flower starts off as a bud and it is fitting that this should be our first attempt at working the flower

The bud is normally a darker shade than the flower; it can be worked with either three or four petals.

You could have an outer layer of three or four green petals to represent the calyx.

MATERIALS (BUD)

❀ *Prepared Thread –Any Colour*
❀ *Copper wire (0.5 and 0.2mm)*
❀ *Silver plated wire (0.25mm)*
❀ *3 Glass beads*
❀ *Floral tape*

MATERIALS (LEAVES)

❀ *Prepared Thread – Green*
❀ *Copper wire (0.5mm and 0.2mm)*
❀ *Floral tape*

METHOD:

With silver plated wire (0.25 mm) and glass beads make the stamens using the method described under Stamen 2 in Section 5.

Cut three pieces of copper wire (0.5mm) each 6 cm in length. With prepared coloured thread, make 3 petals each starting with 9 rounds and using technique described in Section 3. Finish off when each petal is 1.9 cm long.

Cut another three pieces of copper wire (0.5mm) and using green prepared thread make 3 leaves, each starting with 11 rounds, finishing off when leaf is 2cm long.

MOUNTING

Bind the three stamens together using copper wire 0.2mm.

Using tweezers shape petals and place them round stamens, bind tightly and cover with floral tape.

Mount the three leaves using the technique described in Section 4, Group of three leaves – 2nd Method.

Place mounted leaves behind bud, and tightly bind stems together. Cover stem with floral tape and using tweezers, finish off by shaping leaves and petals.

> **Tip.**
>
> *When binding, make sure that stems are tightly bound, slightly spreading wire rounds to ensure that you will not end up with an unduly thick stem.*

One Layered Flower

Figure shows a flower with one layer of petals and three leaves. Having satisfactorily completed the bud, we shall now attempt to make the flower complete with its three leaves.

MATERIALS (FLOWER)

❋ *Prepared Thread – Any colour*
❋ *Copper wire (0.5 and 0.2mm)*
❋ *Silver plated wire (0.25mm)*
❋ *5 glass beads*
❋ *Floral tape*

MATERIALS (LEAVES)

❋ *Prepared Thread – Green*
❋ *Copper wire (0.5mm and 0.2mm)*
❋ *Floral tape*

METHOD

With silver plated wire (0.25mm) and glass beads make 5 stamens.

Cut five pieces of copper wire (0.5mm), each 6cm in length. With prepared coloured thread, make 5 basic petals starting with 5 rounds and using technique described in Section 3. Finish off when each petal is 1.7cm long.

Cut another three pieces of copper wire (0.5mm) each 6cm in length. Make 3 leaves starting with nine rounds and finishing off when 1.9cm long.

MOUNTING

Using copper wire (0.2mm), bind the 5 stamens together.

Shape petals, using tweezers, and place them round

stamens. Bind tightly and cover with floral tape.

Mount the three leaves using 1st or 2nd method described in Section 4.

Hold flower from end of stem and using bent nose pliers bend flower (about 45°)

Place mounted leaves behind flower and tightly bind stems together. Cover stem with floral tape and using tweezers, finish off by shaping leaves and petals.

Bud and five Petals

All you need to make this beautiful flower is three glass beads, eight basic petals and three leaves.

Using the same materials, tools, measurements, and methods we have used so far you should have no difficulty in making this simple flower. However there is a slight difference when mounting.

METHOD

Make bud using the same method described under "Mounting" on page 18.

Place the remaining five petals around bud and bind tightly together, winding copper wire all along the stem.

Cover with floral tape.

Using the same method described under 2nd Method on page 9, mount the three leaves.

Using bent nose pliers bend flower.

Place leaves behind flower and once again bind together by winding copper wire all along the stem.

Finish off by covering with floral tape and using tweezers shape the leaves.

Two Layered Flower

❉ *Five stamens*
❉ *Five basic petals each 1.6cm starting with five rounds for first layer.*
❉ *Seven basic petals each 1.8 cm starting with seven rounds.*
❉ *Copper wire 0.2 for binding.*
❉ *Floral tape.*
❉ *Wire 1mm, 7cm long for anima.*

When mounting flowers with more than one layer it is always better to use stronger stems or anima. Normally 1mm wire is used for this purpose.

Cover about 2cm of anima with floral tape. Bind stamens together by winding 0.2mm wire four or five rounds around stems. DO NOT CUT BINDING WIRE.

Place stamens against anima with beads just touching the top and wind binding wire three to four times. Place first petal against anima just beneath the stamens and bind.

Follow this procedure to individually bind the remaining four petals of the first layer. Wind the binding wire tightly all along petal stems. Cut binding wire.

Make two rounds with binding wire exactly below the first layer. Place the first petal of the second layer just below the first layer and bind.

Using the same procedure described above, individually bind the remaining petals of the second layer.

Make sure that rounds of binding wire do not overlap, as this will give you a thick stem.

Cover anima with floral tape

7 | Project

The Hyacinth

If you have followed the instructions given so far, you are in a position to embark on your first project. This particular project requires time and patience – Do not rush it. The end result is certainly worth the effort put in.

Maria Kerr

MATERIALS

❈ *Prepared Thread*
❈ *Pink Rayon Floss*
❈ *Silver wire 0.25mm*
❈ *Pearls for stamens*
❈ *Copper wire 0.5mm for stems*
❈ *Copper wire 0.2mm for mounting*
❈ *Anima (wire 1.5mm) 14cm long*
❈ *Floral Tape*
❈ *One flower pot 6cm high*
❈ *Five long leaves – Green Rayon Floss*
❈ *30 flowers one layer*

METHOD

Using pearls slightly darker in colour than the thread, make about 90 stamens.

Make about 30 one layered flowers of six basic petals each measuring 1.7cm starting with 9 rounds

Bind three stamens together, place three petals in a triangular pattern around stamens and bind tightly.

22

Place another three petals in the empty spaces and bind tightly till end of stem.

Cover stem with floral tape.

Using the method just described work another twenty-nine flowers.

MOUNTING

Cover anima with floral tape and using copper wire attach one flower to the top of the anima. Cover with floral tape. Using bent nose pliers hold flower next to its base and slightly bend it. Hold flower against anima in such a way that it touches the first flower and bind from a point about 3cms from flower head. Cover binding wire with floral tape. Using the same method mount another four flowers in such a way that all flowers are touching each other and the top one. ***Remember to cover binding wire with floral tape after mounting every flower.***

Bend flower heads slightly more than the first five and using the technique described above attach flowers to anima between those of the previous layer and ensuring that all are touching and no gaps are left.

Do not try to mount flowers in perfect rows and columns – give your work a natural look.

When all flowers are in place slightly bend long leaves and place around anima to "cup" the flowers.

Bind tightly and finish off by covering with floral tape.

POTTING

Check that the completed hyacinth sits nicely in the pot making sure that the anima does not require to be shortened. When satisfied, line sides and base of flowerpot with a piece of thin cardboard, mix a quantity of plaster of Paris and fill about three quarters of pot. Carefully place hyacinth in centre of pot and hold gently until plaster sets.

Finish off by covering top of pot with artificial moss.

Having perfected our basic petal, we shall now learn how to decorate it, thus creating more interesting "species".

The examples shown in this section represent a small number of variations. Use these as a basis to create your own decorated petals.

fig. 8.1

fig 8.2

Figure 8.1 shows a basic petal with a simple decoration. This consists of a farfalla trim to the petals as can be seen in figure 8.2

METHOD

To trim petal, work petal as usual, finishing with two rounds at base of petal. Commence farfalla trim by making two rounds at base of petal followed by two or three rounds of farfalla. Finish of by making two rounds at base of petal, trim and bend wire at top of petal to form hook.

fig 8.3

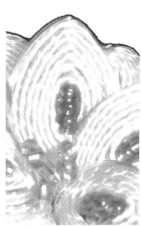

fig 8.4

In figure 8.3, the petals are decorated with a number of glass beads in the centre of the petal that is also trimmed with gold wire. The glass beads will take the place of the usual rounds worked on the stem when starting the petal

METHOD

With the prepared thread make one round on stem and insert three glass beads. With the prepared thread make the usual rounds until the desired length is reached finishing off as usual. If the gold or silver trim is required, follow the technique used to trim with farfalla (See page 24)

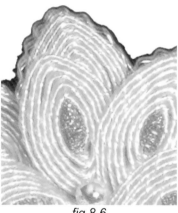

fig 8.5   fig 8.6

Figure 8.5 shows a flower trimmed with farfalla and decorated with ganutell.

METHOD

Follow the same technique used for the previous flower, using a piece of ganutell 0.5cm in length to decorate petal instead of beads. You may use farfalla, gold or silver wire for trimming

fig 8.7   fig 8.8

8 Working with Decorated Basic Petals

METHOD

The flower shown in fig 8.7 has the first layer petals decorated with beads; second layer petals are decorated with glass beads at the tips (fig 8.8). Both layers are decorated with a gold trim

Decorating the first layer of petals should, by now, pose no difficulty.

To decorate the second layer, follow the technique used for the basic petal starting with five rounds. When petal is approximately 1.5cm long, slip bead on stem, make another two rounds and apply trim.

I chose three beautiful shades of yellow to decorate my grandson's holy communion candle.

The square petal is used for making fancy flowers and the Narcissus. The most important part when working the square petal is the beginning and while the explanation is given in detail, we have tried to be as simple and concise as possible.

Upper Left Quadrant	Upper Right Quadrant
Lower Left Quadrant	Lower Right Quadrant

fig 9.1

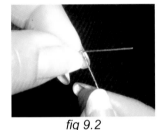

fig 9.2

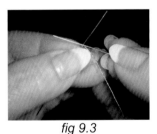

fig 9.3

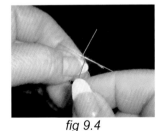

fig 9.4

1. Cut 2 pieces of copper wire (0.5mm), 5cm long and 2.5cm long respectively.

2. Hold the longer piece in a horizontal position and using prepared thread, make one round starting 2cm from the top end (fig. 9.2)

3. Place the shorter piece next to the worked round and across the longer one to form across. Make sure that wires are at right angles. Thread should now be in the left lower quadrant. (fig 9.3)

4. Take thread to the right upper quadrant passing it over the centre of the cross and bring it to the left lower quadrant from the back then passing it over the right short stem.

5. Turn work anti-clockwise to get long stem in a horizontal position. Make one round on the long stem, trapping the starting thread. Trim starting thread. (fig 9.4).

6. Turn work again anti-clockwise so that the long stem is pointing upwards. Make one round on the right short stem.

7. Turn work again anti-clockwise and make one round on the right arm. At this stage the horizontal bar should be firmly bound to the vertical one.

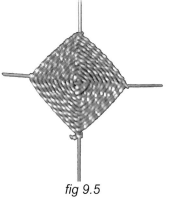

fig 9.5

fig 9.6

8. Turn work anti-clockwise, again making one round on the right arm.

9. Follow this procedure making a round on each successive arm as work is turned anti-clockwise and making sure that rounds are tight.

10. When the desired petal length is reached finish off by working two rounds at the base of the petal (fig 9.5).

11. To complete petal, measure off 4mm from top and sides of petal. Trim and using tweezers bend top and sides backward to form a hook.

If you are certain that you have mastered the square petal, you can now try making a one layered flower.

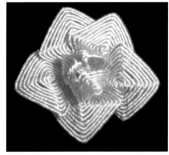

MATERIALS

❋ *Prepared thread*
❋ *Copper wire 0.5mm and 0.2mm.*
❋ *Silver plated wire 0.25mm.*
❋ *Glass beads*
❋ *Floral tape*

METHOD

Using glass beads and silver plated wire make 5 stamens. Instead of the five individual stamens, you may use a seven bead cluster (See Section 5).

With the prepared thread and copper wire make five square petals each 1.6cm long.

MOUNTING

Hold petal in the left hand, place tweezers above the horizontal stem and gently bend petal backwards. Mount flower, finishing off by covering stem with floral tape.

Bud and Five Square Petals

This flower consists of a bud made out of three basic petals sitting on five square petals. Leaves would further enhance the beauty of this flower.

MATERIALS

❋ *Three basic petals each 1.6cm long*
❋ *5 Square petals each 1.8cm long*
❋ *3 glass beads for stamens*

MOUNTING

The same technique as that described on page 20 is used. Remember that the stems of the petals forming the bud should be bound tightly together, winding the 0.2mm copper wire all along the stem. Place the five square petals around the bud. Bind and cover with floral tape.

Two Layered Flower

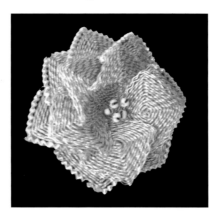

MATERIALS

🌸 *Five square petals each 1.6cm long*
🌸 *Seven square petals each 1.8cm long*
🌸 *Five stamens*

Mount flower.

Decorated Square Petal

The square petal, like the basic petal can be decorated in a number of ways. Apart from the usual trims at the edge, the square petal may be decorated with ganutell, farfalla, beads and rhine stones. When making flowers with more than one layer, the edges of both layers may be decorated, however when decorating the centre of the petal, only the top layer should be decorated.

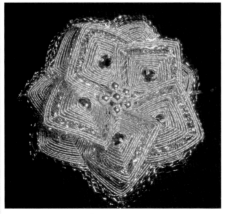

This picture shows a two layered decorated square petal flower.

The edges of the petals are all trimmed with farfalla, the top layer petals have a worked in farfalla border with dark green Rhinestones set in the middle of each petal. The five stamens are encircled with ganutell.

The under side of the rhinestone metal setting should have two channels crossing at right angles to form a cross.

Channels should be wide enough to take a wire 0.5mm thick.

To work a decorated petal cut two pieces of wire 0.5mm, one being 6cm long and the other 3cm.

1. Hold longer stem in left hand and with the prepared thread make one round about 2cm from tip.

2. Slip in rhinestone with back of stone facing you and make one round on top of stone,

3. Pass shorter piece through channel and make one round on right arm.

4. Turn work anticlockwise and again make one round next to starting round, trapping end of prepared thread. Trim protruding thread. At this stage, the cross is not secure and work should be handled carefully.

5. Turn again anticlockwise and once again make one round on right arm. Cross should now be somewhat secure.

6. Follow this procedure until the desired length is reached. In this particular case make eight rounds finishing at the bottom of the longer stem. DO NOT CUT PREPARED THREAD.

7. Holding work in left hand, with longer stem held horizontally and with base of petal on right hand side, make one round with farfalla starting where you have finished off with the prepared thread. Turn anticlockwise and make one round on right arm.

8. Turn again anticlockwise and make one round on right stem.

9. Follow this procedure until you reach the farfalla starting point.

10. Lay prepared thread against stem and with farfalla,

make one round securing thread to stem.

11. Following this procedure work round the petal once or twice, remembering to work round on stem and thread every time the starting point is reached. DO NOT CUT FARFALLA.

12. Turn work anticlockwise and with prepared thread work one round on right arm. Follow procedure and go three times around petal making sure that farfalla is lying against stem and that rounds secure the farfalla to stem.

13. On completion of the third round finish off by making two rounds at the base of petal and trim thread.

14. Turn work anticlockwise and with farfalla make two rounds on the right arm. Continue working in this manner going around the petal twice.

15. Finish off by making two rounds at the base of petal and trim. Using tweezers, bend tip backwards to form a hook.

Cupped Square Petal Flower

The petals of this flower are identical to those of the square petal described on page 28; the only difference is that the petals are shaped before mounting the flower to give it a "cupped" appearance. The petals should not be decorated,

However edges may be trimmed.

To shape the petal, hold it between the third finger and thumb and gently press down forefinger over the length of the petal, bending it slightly.

MATERIALS

❀ *Green Rayon Floss for leaves*
❀ *Ivory Rayon Floss for flower*
❀ *Yellow Rayon Floss for flower*
❀ *Silver or green wire 0.6mm for leaves*
❀ *Copper wire 0.5mm and 0.2mm for leaves and flower*
❀ *Silver wire 0.25mm for flower*
❀ *Gold wire 0.25mm for flower*
❀ *Ready made pearl stamens*
❀ *Anima 1mm about 15cm long*
❀ *Floral tape*
❀ *One Flower pot 6cm high*

METHOD

The picture shows a pot with five stems. There is a bud, two flowers and three long leaves on every stem or anima. The instructions that follow show how we can make a complete anima. The number of petals and leaves we have to work depends on the number of anima we would like to have in our pot.

For the bud make 3 basic petals each 2cms long starting with 9 rounds. Use thread number 30746 and 0.25mm silver wire.

Make 2 flowers each with:
    2 square petals, 1.9 cm, using yellow thread and gold wire 0.25mm.

6 basic petals 1.9cms starting with 9 rounds, using the ivory thread and silver wire 0.25mm.

6 ready made pearl stamens for each flower.

Make three or five long leaves using the green thread and the method described in Section 4 – Leaves.

MOUNTING Mount bud not forgetting the three stamens. Stem should be covered with floral tape.

The narcissus is made of a short cylinder sitting on six basic petals. To make the mounting easier to understand we shall refer to these parts as "cup and saucer". The "cup" is made up of two square petals that are shaped in the form of a cylinder.

To shape the cup hold from stem and bend petal in the

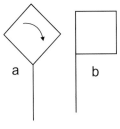

direction of arrow (a) to form a "flag"(b). Hold the petal in a horizontal position as shown in diagram c of fig 11.1. Holding petal along the upper edge with tweezers, apply slight pressure to bend petal, giving it the shape of a half cylinder (d).

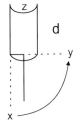

Hold stem and with tweezers bend stem "x" in the direction of arrow to "y". At "z" mid-point of half-cylinder bend stem again so that stem is now protruding from centre of the half-cylinder. With the other square petal, make another half cylinder.

fig 11.1

Bind six stamens. Place between the two half cylinders and bind stems tightly together. Making the "saucer" is somewhat easier. Bind three basic petals, in the form of a triangle to the "cup" leaving a space of 4mm from the bottom of the cup.(See fig. 11.2). Place the remaining three petals in the empty spaces, binding tightly every petal. Cover stem with floral tape.

fig 11.2

Using same technique, work the second flower.

Having made the bud, flowers and leaves, we shall now mount them on the anima.

Cover anima with floral tape.

Place bud over anima in such a way that the base of the bud is about 2cm above the top of the anima. Using 0.2mm copper wire, bind bud to anima and cover with floral tape.

Using bent nose bend flower just over 90° from below the "saucer". Bind flower from a point 2cm below the bud, cover with floral tape.

Once again bend second flower and bind flower 0.5cm below first flower and facing the opposite direction. Cover with floral tape.

Bind first long leaf at a point 6cm below second flower and cover with floral tape.

Bind second leaf 4cm below first leaf and third leaf about 2 cm lower down. Remember to bind with floral tape every time you bind a leaf.

POTTING

Make the desired number of anima, it is strongly suggested that anima are not of equal length to ensure that flowers are not at the same level.

Loosely bind the anima together and follow the technique described on page 22 of Section 7.

Detail from Lilium Mount.

The T petal is worked in nearly the same way as the square petal, the only difference being that about halfway through the work no rounds are made on the upper arm of the cross. This produces a petal with a rounded top that lends itself beautifully to make the pine cone and the queen of flowers – the Rose.

METHOD

To work the petal follow the same method described in Section 9 – The Square Petal, up to paragraph 8, now turn petal anti-clockwise and work round on right arm.

Turn petal again anti-clockwise and make round over the right arm.

Once again turn petal anti-clockwise. The longer stem should be now in a horizontal position with the short arm on the right hand side. Pass thread over the arm without making a round, placing thread snugly against worked rounds and turning work anti-clockwise make round on right arm.

Follow this procedure until the desired petal length is reached, making sure that at this stage no rounds are made on the upper arm of the cross.

Shades of Autumn.

13 The Rose

The rose is a combination of basic and T petals. The colours that are commonly used are red, pink, yellow, ivory and blue. Leaves are worked in groups of five, and a detailed description of how to mount the leaves can be found on page 9.

MATERIALS

❋ *Prepared thread, two colours, pink or any preferred colour for flower and green for leaves*
❋ *Copper wire (0.5 and 0.2mm)*
❋ *Silver plated wire (0.25mm)*
❋ *3 glass beads*
❋ *Anima (1mm) 15cm long*
❋ *Floral tape*

METHOD

With silver plated wire and glass beads make three stamens as described in Stamen 2 of Section 5.

With prepared green thread, make 15 basic petals for the leaves, 12 starting with 11 rounds and finishing off when leaf is 2cm long and 3 leaves starting with nine rounds and finishing off when 1.9 cm long.

With prepared coloured thread make 3 basic petals for the bud each starting with five rounds. Finish off when each basic petal is 1.7cm long.

Using coloured thread make 5 T petals each 1.9cm and another 7 T petals each 2.1cm. Shape all the petals using the technique described on page 33, under "Cupped Square Petal Flower".

MOUNTING

Use the same technique described on page 21 to mount the bud. Remember that the stems of the petals forming the bud should be bound tightly together by winding the 0.2mm copper wire all along the stem. Add the two layers of petals binding tightly every petal.

Having mounted the three groups of five leaves, place the first group at about 3cm from the base of the rose, again binding tightly with copper wire and cover with floral tape. Bend the leaves outward from the stem at an angle of approximately 45° Place the second group of 5 leaves 3.5cm further down from the first group and repeat the process making sure that this second group is not directly below the first group but to the right of it. Place the last group 4 cm further down from the second group and to the left of the first. Repeat binding process.

The Kite Petal

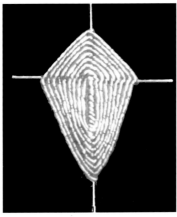

Apart from making fancy flowers, this petal is also used to make the Tiger Lily, the Calla Lily and the Star of Bethlehem. When making fancy flowers, the petals may be decorated with ganutell, farfalla, gold and silver trims and beads.

The technique to work this kite shaped petal is very similar to that used for the Square Petal, however the end result is a petal with its lower half longer than the upper half.

METHOD

To make the kite petal, use the same method described in Section 9 - The Square Petal, however when coming to paragraph 2, you should make five rounds, instead of one, starting your rounds 3cm from the top and working upwards. It is the extra number of rounds that give the petal the longer lower half.

The focal point of a mount under a glass dome.

15 Fancy Flowers with the Kite Petal

The picture shows a two-layered fancy flower made with the kite petal. The first layer consists of five petals, while six petals form the second layer.

MATERIALS

❀ Prepared Thread
❀ Copper wire 0.2mm and 0.5mm
❀ Gold plated wire 0.25mm
❀ Gold glass beads
❀ Rhinestone
❀ Ganutell
❀ Floral Tape

METHOD

Using rhinestone and Ganutell and using technique described in Section 5 – paragraph Stamen 5, make stamen.

Make 5 decorated kite petals starting with 9 rounds. When petal measures 1.5cm slip a gold glass bead in the upper part of the stem, work one round and again slip a second bead on upper stem, make another round ending work at the base by making two rounds round stem. Using gold plated 0.25mm wire, work two rounds.

Make 6 decorated kite petals starting with 11 rounds. When petal measures 1.6cm slip a gold bead on the upper and left and right arm. Make one round and again slip bead on the upper arm ONLY. Make one round finishing off by making two rounds at the bottom of the stem. Make two rounds using gold plated wire.

To shape, hold petal upright with the right side facing you, place tweezers above horizontal arm and gently bend backwards to make an angle of nearly 90°.

MOUNTING

Starting with the first layer (5 petals), use tweezers, to slightly bend stems at the base of the petal, place petal in front of rhinestone so that bent petal is facing inwards, bind tightly, repeat this procedure for the four remaining petals.

To mount the 6 petals which form the second layer, use the procedure used for mounting the first layer, however this time the bent petals must be facing outwards. Finish off by covering the stem with floral tape

The picture shows a different version of the flower we have just worked. The only difference lies in the mounting and stamens.

Instead of a rhinestone decorated with ganutell, three silver pearls were used. To make the stamen, refer to Section 5 – Stamens. The petal is decorated in exactly the same way as the previous flower, the only difference being that silver beads are used instead of gold beads.

MOUNTING

Use the same method described above, however when mounting the first layer make sure that the bent petal is facing outwards.

The figure shows a bunch of four tiger lilies complete with long leaves. The following instructions will help you make this arrangement.

To turn this small bunch into an interesting project, work more flowers and leaves.

MATERIALS

❀ *Green Rayon Floss for leaves*
❀ *Ivory and Shades of Pink Rayon Floss flowers*
❀ *Green cardboard for leaves*
❀ *Copper wire 0.5mm and 0.2mm.*
❀ *Silver Ganutell for stamens*
❀ *Silver wire 0.25mm*
❀ *Anima 1mm, 10cm long*
❀ *Floral tape*

15 Fancy Flowers with the Kite Petal

Using green thread and cardboard make four long leaves following one of the methods described In Section 4 – Leaves.

Cut silver ganutell into 24 pieces each 8mm long. Follow the technique described under Stamen 6 in Section 5 to make four bunches of stamens with 6 loops in each bunch.

Using a different colour for every six petals, make 24 kite petals each 2.2cm long starting with 6 rounds. Refer to Section 14 – The Kite petal.

Using usual technique, mount the four flowers.

1. Bind a leaf to each flower covering stem with floral tape. If you intend turning this arrangement into a project it is recommended that you have three leaves to every flower.

2. Cover anima with floral tape.

3. Bind the ivory flower and leaf tightly to the anima, winding the .02mm wire all along the stem. Cover with floral tape.

4. In the same manner, bind the next flower and leaf slightly below and to the right of the ivory flower. Once again cover with floral tape.

5. Place the third flower below the first and just touching the first and second flower. Bind and cover with floral tape.

6. Repeat the process, with the fourth flower just touching the second and third flower.

The Kite T Petal is so called because it is a combination of the Kite and the T petal with a triangular lower part and a rounded top.

This particular petal is used to make the hibiscus and a few other flowers including the amaryllis.

METHOD

Begin this petal in the same way as the Square petal described in Section 9, however when coming to paragraph 2 you should make 9 or more rounds. The petal in the figure starts with over twelve rounds. Follow the procedure for the square petal up to paragraph 8, now turn petal anti-clockwise and make round on right arm. Turn petal again anti-clockwise and make a round over the right arm.

Once again turn petal anti-clockwise. The longer stem should be now in a horizontal position with the short arm on the right hand side. Pass thread over the arm without making a round, placing thread snugly against worked rounds and turning work anti-clockwise make round on right arm.

Follow this procedure until the desired petal length is reached, making sure that at this stage no rounds are made on the upper arm of the cross.

The hibiscus flower can be found in a variety of colours, the most common being red, orange, and yellow. Cream flowers may also be found.

MATERIALS

The materials listed are for one flower. Make any number of flowers you want and display in a small vase.

* *Prepared thread, red and green*
* *5 Red glass beads and about 30 yellow glass beads*
* *Gold wire 0.25mm for stamens*
* *Gold plated wire 0.6mm, 5cm long*
* *Copper wire 0.5mm and 0.2mm*
* *Anima 1mm, 12cm long*
* *Floral Tape*

METHOD

With prepared red thread make 5 kite T petals starting with 13 rounds and finishing off when 2.5 cm long. Shape petals.

Using the green prepared thread make nine basic petals for leaves:

3 - 1.7cm long starting with six rounds.
3 - 1.9cm long starting with seven rounds.
3 - 2.1cm long starting with nine rounds.

Cover all leaves with floral tape.

Using 0.25 gold wire bead individually all glass beads

MOUNTING

Cover anima with floral tape.

Bind the five red glass beads to the 0.6mm wire so that beads are about 1cm higher than gold wire. Wind the binding wire neatly for half a centimetre. so that rounds lie against each other.

Using tweezers hold two yellow beads together 1cm away from beads, place over the gold wire so that tweezers are in line with the gold binding wire. Again wind wire neatly for about half a centimetre. Repeat the process until all yellow beads are used, binding beads spirally along the gold (0.6mm) wire.

Bind stamens to anima using 0.2mm copper wire.

Bind the five kite T petals one at a time to the stamens, making sure that stamens protrude above the petals. Cover with floral tape.

Approximately 2cm below base of flower, bind the smallest leaf (1.7cm) and cover with floral tape, turn the flower slightly and bind another leaf (1.7cm) at about 1cm below the first leaf, again covering with floral tape. Using the same procedure bind the remaining leaves.

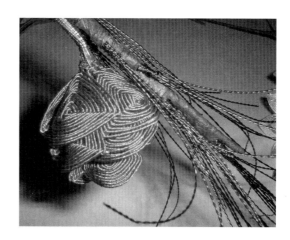

Use the T petal to make this simple yet attractive pinecone. The pine can be used as part of a Christmas decoration project or on its own to decorate a Christmas tree.

MATERIALS

❋ Prepared thread made with:
❋ Brown Rayon Floss or brown metallic thread and copper coloured wire.
❋ Brown wire 0.5mm
❋ Brown wire 0.25mm or 0.2mm
❋ Green wire 0.25mm
❋ Anima 1mm 6 cm long
❋ Brown floral tape

METHOD

Using brown wire 0.5mm and prepared thread, make

3 T petals each 1.7cm long
5 T petals each 1.9cm long
5 T petals each 2.1cm long

Cut a 1m length of green wire, place middle over spindle hook, bring ends together and twist. This should be enough to form a bunch of needles made up of 2 lengths of 4cm, 2 of 5cm, 2 of 6cm and 2 of 7cm. You will need six bunches.

Cover 1mm Anima with brown floral tape.

MOUNTING

Shape petals using method described on page 33 under "Cupped Square Petal Flower". When shaping, the wrong side of the petal should be facing you.

On a piece of wire 0.5mm about 6 cm long, bind the 3 x 1.7mm petals one at a time. Petals should overlap.

Pine and Needles

Place the base of a 1.9cm petal 0.5cm lower than the base of the previous petals and bind. Overlap and bind the remaining four petals.

Once again placing the 2.1cm petals 0.5cm lower than the previous ones, overlap and bind tightly.

Cover with rounds of brown wire, rounds should lie neatly against each other.

Place the bottom ends of a bunch of needles together and using brown wire neatly bind tightly together leaving a length of about 15cm of brown wire. Bind the remaining bunches in the same way.

Place the first bunch at the tip of the 1mm anima, slightly overlapping and using the 15cm length, bind tightly and neatly together. (Remaining lengths of this 15cm length should not be cut off but are to be used together with the 15cm lengths of the next bunch of needles). Make sure that the binding rounds are tight and lie next to each other. Place the second bunch about 0.5cm from the bottom of the first but NOT directly beneath it and again bind tightly. In the same manner bind three of the remaining four bunches.

Bend slightly the stem of the pine and bind it to the anima, making use of the remains of the 15cm lengths of binding wire.

Bind the remaining bunch of needles below the pine, ensuring that binding rounds are tight and lie next to each other.

More needles and cones can be added.

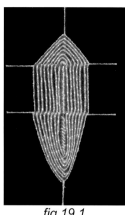

fig 19.1

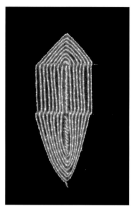

fig 19.2

✤ *Green Rayon Floss and Green wire 0.2mm for prepared thread*
✤ *Green copper wire 0.5mm*

1. Cut one piece green copper wire 0.5mm, 7 cm long and two pieces each 3cm long.

2. Hold long stem in left hand, place prepared thread against stem and at about 3.5cm from the top make eleven rounds.

3. Place one of the shorter stems next to the worked rounds and across the long stem to make a cross.

4. Prepared thread should now be in the right lower quadrant. Take thread over the small stem into the left upper quadrant. And make eleven round on the upper stem.

5. Place the second shorter stem next to the worked eleven rounds and across the long stem, forming a second cross.

6. Prepared thread should now be in the right lower quadrant. Take thread over the small stem into the left upper quadrant. Work one round on the upper part of the stem.

7. Now, make one round on the right upper arm and turn work anticlockwise making one round on the right lower arm.

8. Take thread to the starting rounds and make one round, trapping the starting thread.

9. Turn work anticlockwise and make one round on the

19 The Double Kite Petal

upper part of the left arm.

10. Carry thread forward and make one round on the upper part of the right arm.

11. Make one round on the upper part of the long stem.

12. Turn anticlockwise and repeat process until work measures 3.3cm.

13. When the desired length is reached, measure off 4mm from top of leaf at vertical stem and on either side of the horizontal stems, cut off remaining length. (fig 19.1)

14. Using tweezers bend the protruding top part of the stem and of horizontal arms to form hooks (fig. 19.2)

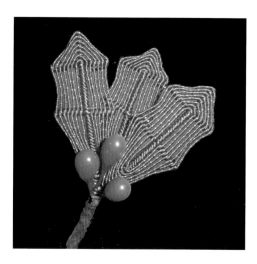

MATERIALS

* *Green Rayon Floss and green wire 0.2mm. for prepared thread.*
* *Green wire 0.5mm.*
* *Copper wire 0.2mm.*
* *3 Red berries – ready made.*
* *Floral tape.*

METHOD

Using green prepared thread make 3 double kite petals.

Shape the three petals by gently pressing the middle section with tweezers, giving the leaf the shape seen in the figure.

Bind tightly the three berries using 0.2mm copper wire.

Bind the three leaves together.

Place berries over leaves and bind neatly.

Cover with floral tape.

Focal point of a headdress:
Three flowers made out of silver lined glass beads on spiral wire.

The Y petal is so called because it is made on a Y shaped frame.

Y petals can be flat shaped or frilled. Both petals are made on the same principle, and the differences between the two shall be dealt with in this Section.

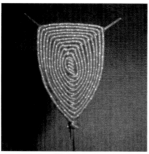

| *Fig 19.1* | *Fig 19.2* | *Fig 19.3* |

Flat Shaped Y Petal

MATERIALS

✤ *Prepared Thread.*
✤ *1 piece copper wire 0.5mm, 2.5cm long.*
✤ *1 piece copper wire 0.5mm, 5cm long.*

METHOD

1. Place the top ends of the two pieces of copper wire together, holding them in the left hand from the bottom end of the short piece.

2. Lay the prepared thread against the two pieces of wire, holding it between forefinger and thumb.

3. Working upwards, make five rounds.

4. Turn work anti-clockwise bring thread forward and make one round, trapping prepared thread.

5. Turn work once again anticlockwise and open the arms to form an angle of 90°.

6. Bring thread forward, make one round on the left arm cross over to right arm and make one round, turn work anticlockwise and make one round.

7. Repeat this process until the desired length is reached (fig. 19.1)

8. To complete petal, measure off 4mm from top corners of petal and cut off remaining length. Using tweezers, bend top parts of stem backwards to form a hook. (fig

19.2)

9. To shape petal, hold it from the base and placing tweezers across and nearly over the V, bend backwards. (fig 19.3)

Frilled Shaped Y Petals

The frilled Y petal is worked in exactly the same way as the flat shaped Y petal the only difference being in paragraphs 3,5 and 9.

When paragraph 3 is reached, a least nine rounds should be worked to give the petal a more triangular look.

When paragraph 5 is reached, the arms should be opened in nearly a straight line, giving the petal a longer edge and making it possible to give it a frilly shape.

To shape petal, hold it from the base and placing tweezers along left edge, bend to the back. Again place tweezers along right edge and bend to the front. This will give the petal a wavy or frilly look.

The picture shows a two-layered fancy flower made with the flat shaped Y Petal.

All the petals have been decorated with two rounds of gold farfalla.

* ❋ *Prepared thread with Yellow Rayon Floss and gold wire 0.2mm*
* ❋ *Gold farfalla*
* ❋ *Copper wire 0.5mm and 0.2mm*
* ❋ *Silver wire 0.25mm*
* ❋ *Seven glass beads*
* ❋ *Anima 1mm, 7cm long*
* ❋ *Floral tape*

Using silver wire 0.25mm and glass beads make cluster as described in Stamen 4 on page 15.

Make 5 flat shaped Y Petals trimmed with farfalla each 2cm long starting with 11 rounds and another seven petals each 2.3cm long starting with 13 rounds. To trim flowers with farfalla see Section 8 "Working with Decorated Basic Petals" Page 24.

Cover about 2cm of anima with floral tape.

Place stamen against anima with cluster just over the top of the anima and bind tightly together.

To mount the flower, follow instructions given under "Mounting" on page 21.

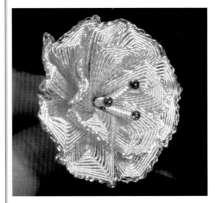

Two layered fancy flower made with the frilled shaped Y Petal.

The petals have been trimmed with gold farfalla. Gold ganutell and blue glass beads were used for the stamens.

Working with the Y Petal

🌸 *Prepared thread made with two shades of Yellow of Rayon Floss together with gold wire 0.2mm*
🌸 *Gold farfalla*
🌸 *Copper wire 0.5mm and 0.2mm*
🌸 *Silver wire 0.5mm and 0.2mm*
🌸 *Silver wire 0.25mm*
🌸 *6 blue glass beads*
🌸 *3 pieces ganutell each 1cm long*
🌸 *Anima 1mm, 7cm. long*
🌸 *Floral tape*

To make the stamens. Cut a piece of silver wire, 0.25mm, 10cm long.

Bead a blue glass bead in the middle of the wire, bring ends together and pass them through a 1cm length of ganutell and through another glass bead.

Pass one of the ends again through the blue bead as shown in the figure and twist wires together.

Make 5 frilled shaped Y petals trimmed with farfalla each 2cm long starting with 9 rounds and another 9 petals each 2.3cm starting with 11 rounds, using the darker shade to make the 5 petals. When making petals remember that the arms should be opened as wide as possible.

Cover about 2cm of the anima with floral tape.

Place stamens against anima with the bottom beads just over the top of the anima and bind tightly together.

To mount the flower follow the instructions given under "Mounting" on page 21.

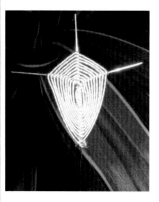

At a glance the three-stemmed petal may be mistaken for a Y Petal. Closer examination shows that the petal has a rib running down between the two arms.

❀ *Prepared thread*
❀ *Copper wire 0.5mm*

1. Cut one piece copper wire 0.5mm, 6cm long and another two pieces each 3cm long.

2. Place the three pieces together and holding them between forefinger and thumb in a horizontal position work 7 rounds starting about 2.5 cm. from the top.

3. Turn work anticlockwise and make one round to trap starting thread.

4. Again turn work anti-clockwise bring thread forward and open arms as shown in diagram.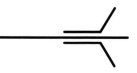

5. Make one round on upper arm, then on middle arm followed by round on remaining arm,

6. Turn work anticlockwise, bring thread forward and make one round.

7. Again turn work anticlockwise, bringing thread forward and once again work one round on the upper arm, the middle arm and the lower arm.

8. Repeat paragraphs 6 and 7 until the desired length is reached. Using tweezers bend top of arms backwards to form a hook.

24 Working With the Three Stemmed Petal

This fancy flower trimmed with silver farfalla is made with flat shaped three stemmed petals. The stamen is a blue rhine stone decorated with ganutell.

MATERIALS

* *Prepared thread made with blue Rayon Floss and blue copper wire 0.2mm*
* *Silver farfalla*
* *Copper wire 0.5mm*
* *Silver wire 0.25mm*
* *Blue rhinestone*
* *Silver ganutell*
* *Anima 1mm, 7cm long*
* *Floral tape*

METHOD

Using blue rhinestone, 0.25mm silver wire and ganutell, follow the instructions in Section 5 Stamens in paragraph "Stamen 5" to make the stamens

Use .05mm copper wire to make 5 flat shaped, three stemmed petals trimmed with silver farfalla each 2cm long, starting with 9 rounds and another seven petals each 2.3cm long starting with 11 rounds.

To trim with farfalla follow instructions in Section 8 "Working with Decorated Basic Petals" on page 24.

To shape petals follow the instructions in Section21 "The Y Petal" paragraph 9 on page 56.

MOUNTING

Cover about 2 cm of anima with floral tape.

Place stamen against anima with rhinestone just above top of anima and bind tightly together. To mount flower follow instructions on page 21.

24 Working With the Three Stemmed Petal

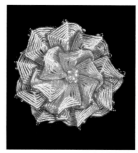

Another fancy flower made with three stemmed petals.

The frilled petal is used and all petals are trimmed with two rounds of blue coloured copper wire.

MATERIALS

* *Prepared thread made with acqua Rayon Floss and blue copper wire 0.2mm.*
* *Copper wire 0.5mm.*
* *Silver wire 0.25mm.*
* *7 Blue glass Beads.*
* *Anima 1mm, 7cm long.*
* *Floral tape.*

METHOD

Using the .025mm copper wire and glass beads, make seven stamens, following instructions in Section 5, paragraph Stamen 2.

Make 6 frilled three stemmed petals trimmed with two rounds of blue wire 0.2mm, each 2.1cm long, starting with 9 rounds and another 9 petals each 2.3cm, starting with 11 rounds.

To trim with wire follow instructions in Section 8 "Working with Decorated Basic Petals" on page 24.

Shape petals according to instructions in Section 21 "The Y Petal" , the last paragraph on page 56

MOUNTING

Cover about 2cm of anima with floral tape.

Place stamens against anima with glass beads just above top of anima and bind tightly together. To mount flower follow instructions on page 21.

A decorated comb makes an ideal headdress for a bridesmaid.

Apart from being used for the butterfly wing, this particular petal is used to make fancy flowers

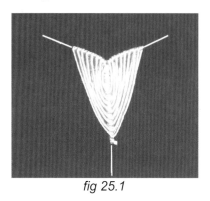

fig 25.1   fig 25.2

MATERIALS

❋ *Prepared Thread.*
❋ *1 piece copper wire 0.5mm, 3cm long*
❋ *1 piece copper wire 0.5mm, 6cm long.*

METHOD

1. Place the top ends of the two pieces of copper wire together, holding them in the left hand from the bottom end of the short piece.

2. Lay the prepared thread against the two pieces of wire, holding it between forefinger and thumb.

3. Working upwards, make nine rounds.

4. Turn work anti-clockwise bring thread forward and make one round, trapping prepared thread.

5. Turn work once again anticlockwise, open up arms to an angle of slightly less than 180° and make two rounds on upper arm.

6. Turn petal back to front, so that the Y part is held between forefinger and thumb, bring thread forward and work one round.

7. Turn work anticlockwise bring thread forward and make two rounds on upper arm

8. Again turn petal back to front, so that the Y part is held between forefinger and thumb, bring thread forward and work one round.

9. Again turn work anticlockwise bring thread forward and make two rounds on upper arm.

10. Repeat the process of turning petal back to front (paragraph 8) and turning work anti clockwise

25 The Butterfly Wing Petal

(paragraph 9) until the desired length is reached. The butterfly petal is measured from the bottom of the V to the base.

11. Using tweezers bend the top parts of the two arms to form a hook (fig 25.2).

❀ *Prepared thread made with pink Rayon Floss and pink copper wire 0.2mm.*
❀ *Gold farfalla.*
❀ *Copper wire 0.2mm.*
❀ *Silver wire 0.25mm.*
❀ *15 gold coloured glass beads.*
❀ *Anima 1mm, 7cm long.*
❀ *Floral tape.*

Using silver wire 0.25mm and glass beads make three stamens by beading 5 glass beads together for each stamen.

Make 5 butterfly wing petals trimmed with 2 rounds of gold farfalla each 1.8cm long starting with seven rounds, and another 7 petals each 2cm long starting with nine rounds.

To trim petals follow instructions in Section 8, "Working with Decorated Basic Petals".

Cover about 2cm of anima with floral tape and mount flower in the usual way.

MATERIALS

❀ Prepared thread
❀ Silver wire 0.5mm for stems of petals
❀ Silver wire 0.4mm and 0.25mm
❀ Silver ganutell 2.5mm and 1.5mm
❀ 1 Pearl 5mm and 20 glass beads same colour

METHOD

Make 2 Basic petals 2cms with 5 glass beads in centre of petal and 2 Butterfly Wing petals 1.9cms decorated with glass beads

Cut 3 pieces of ganutell 2.5mm, 4.5cm long and twist each of **two** lengths on a piece of 0.4 mm silver wire 10cm long.

Cut 2 pieces of silver ganutell 1.5mm, 4.5cm long

MOUNTING

<u>The thorax or body.</u>

1. Through the end loops of the 2 pieces of twisted ganutell, pass a piece of wire 0.4mm, 12cm long. Bring ends of wire together and twist neatly about 2.5cm from loops, making sure that the remaining length is not twisted together.
2. Slip the 1.5mm ganutell piece over this remaining length, bend over itself so that it lies over the other two pieces of ganutell.
3. Using .25mm silver wire join the two lengths of twisted wire protruding from the ganutell pieces by making three or four rounds.
4. Neatly finish off by bending backs the twisted wires to form a small hook. Trim if hook is too large. Attached

to the body there should be only two pieces of .04mm silver wire that will form the antennae or feelers.

The Feelers

5. Slip the pearl over the two wires, pushing it in gently as far as it will go.

6. Shape feelers by pulling gently outwards to form a V.

7. Slip a piece of 1.5mm ganutell over each feeler and finish off by inserting a glass bead over the ganutell.

8. Bend the protruding wire over the bead and trim.

The Wings.

9. Place a basic petal against the butterfly wing petal with the right side of the basic petal against the wrong side of the butteflywing petal and with bentnose pliers carefully twist the two stems together till the end.

10. Using the other two petals, make a mirror image of the wing

11. Insert both pairs of twisted stem, in slot between ganutell, close to the head.

12. Using 0.25mm wire bind tightly, close to the body the two twisted stems ending with two or three rounds around the body

13. The twisted stems make up the legs. Cut legs about 2cm. long and separate to form an inverted V.

14. Bend 3mm from end of leg and bend at an angle of 90°.

15. Shape wings so that the basic petal is under the butterfly wing petal.

Samples made from different materials and using different techniques.

Chenille is a tufty velvety cord made from rayon twist and used for making leaves, flowers and fillers. To make Chenille a flat piece of cane about 35cm long and 0.5cm wide slightly tapered at one end is required.

* *One piece of rayon twist 140cm long (or four times the length of the cane)*

* *One piece of Silver, gold or coloured copper wire 0.25cm, 35 cm long (or equal to the length of the cane)*

Cane

1. Fold the length of rayon twist in half and then fold once more in half.

2. Fold the length of wire in half.

3. Place wire over the thread and knot firmly together.

4. Pass tapered part of cane through the wire loop, holding knot on the outside bottom part of the cane. For 12 stitches you may start working 8cm away from tapered point.

5. Hold wire back and with the thread make one round over the cane.

6. Holding rayon between forefinger and thumb, hook wire with two fingers, pull tight and pass loop below the cane, twist to trap thread.

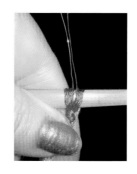

7. Keeping wire loop tight, return loop to original position. Make sure not too pull too strongly on loop as this may break the wire.

8. Follow procedures from paragraph 5 to 8 until the required length is reached.

9. Finish off by passing remaining thread through loop, twist wire and again pass thread through loop. Repeat four or five times.

10. Slide chenille out of the cane

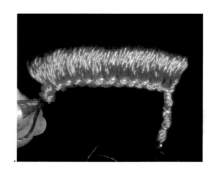

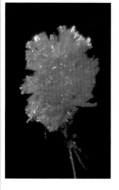

1. Cut a piece of wire 0.5mm, 6cm long, place against starting knot and bind firmly using 0.2mm wire.

2. Fold mid-way bringing end next to starting knot and bind firmly and trim.

3. Depending on what the chenille is being used for, it may be either left looped or else loops may be cut and trimmed.

The chenille may be used as filler, especially when making large mounts and can also be used to make a variety of flowers. When green thread is used these chenille petals may be used to make leaves.

MATERIALS

❊ Rayon Twist - Red
❊ Red and gold coloured copper wire 0.25mm
❊ Copper wire 0.2mm
❊ Ganutell about 2cms long. (Length depends on the circumference of the gold pearl)
❊ Gold pearl
❊ Floral tape
❊ Anima 1mm, 6cm long.

METHOD

Make stamen by threading the piece of ganutell, with gold wire and using the technique described in Stamen 5 on page 15 to decorate gold pearl.

Make 5 chenille petals each with twelve stitches. When complete cut loops of each petal and trim.

Cover about 2cm of anima with floral tape

Place stamen against anima with gold pearl just over the top of the anima and bind tightly together.

MOUNTING

Mount the flower in the usual way if you have any difficulties follow instructions given under "Mounting" on page 21.

Pom-poms (one cut and one looped)

The two pom-poms shown in the photograph are made in exactly the same manner. To get the effect of the flower on the left, the loops of the completed flower are be cut and trimmed.

MATERIALS

For each flower:

❀ *Rayon Twist – Peach.*
❀ *Gold coloured copper wire 0.25mm.*
❀ *Copper wire 0.2mm.*
❀ *Ganutell about 2cms long.*
❀ *Gold pearl.*
❀ *Floral tape.*
❀ *Anima 1mm, 6cm long.*

METHOD

Thread gold wire through ganutell and decorate the gold pearl, following the instructions given on page 15, under Stamen 5.

Make sixteen chenille stitches on cane, slide out of cane.

MOUNTING

1. Cover about 2cm of anima with floral tape.
2. Place stamen against anima with gold pearl just over the top of anima and bind tightly together.
3. Place starting knot against anima, underneath the gold pearl and using 0.2mm copper wire bind together making three rounds. Do not cut wire.
4. Turn chenille round anima but do NOT tighten.
   The gold pearl should now be embedded in the chenille.
5. Using the attached copper wire, bind end of chenille to anima, trim and cover with floral tape.

Pom-Pom flower with leaves

The pom-pom, may either be left looped (flower on right on previous page) or loops can be cut and trimmed (flower on left on previous page).

The flower in the picture can be made by combining five pom-poms. This flower is decorated with chenille leaves.

MATERIALS

❀ *Rayon Twist – Bright yellow for flower and green for leaves.*
❀ *Gold and green coloured copper wire 0.25mm.*
❀ *Copper Wire 0.2mm. and 0.5mm*
❀ *1 Gold pearl and 11 pearls – natural colour.*
❀ *Floral tape.*
❀ *Anima 1mm, 6 cm long.*

METHOD

Using one gold, six pearls and gold copper wire 0.25mm, make cluster as described in Stamen 4 on page 15.

Using the remaining five pearls and 0.25mm gold copper wire make five individual stamens.

Make 5 separate pom-poms, using a pearl as the stamens and mounting it on a length of 0.5mm wire.

MOUNTING

1. Cover about 2cm of anima with floral tape.
1. Place stamen against anima with cluster just over the top of the anima and bind tightly together.
2. Bind tightly the five pom-poms, one at a time to the anima, using the 0.2cm copper wire.
3. Finish off by covering anima with floral tape.

Simply Beautiful

Beautiful flowers can be made using spiral wire, locally known as Molla. Spiral wire is very similar to a type of beading wire and is bought in lengths. When buying spiral wire care should be taken to make sure that you are supplied with the right material. Beading wire may be used as a substitute but the end result would be far from perfect.

The spiral wire is shaped into petals or leaves and the resulting framework is filled with either a strand of Rayon silk thread from which a ply has been teased out or very fine metallic thread or even with Ganutell

The technique is simple enough, a length of spiral wire is gently stretched so that the spirals are slightly separated. Apply the same tension throughout making sure that the distances between spirals are the same. How far apart the spirals should be depends very much on the medium used to fill the framework.

Never cut the required pieces of spiral wire and then stretch them individually. This is a very common mistake and should be avoided.

Making Petals with Spiral Wire

MATERIALS

Thread: The thread used to fill the spiral wire frame is rayon floss, however this also requires a certain amount of preparation. The very first thing that was discussed in this book was how to tease out the six strands of a rayon floss skein. To fill in a spiral wire frame cut a length of 75cm from a rayon floss strand. The strand is made out *of two-ply. Using the same technique used to tease out the strands, slightly dampen the cut length and tease out one ply.*

❀ *1 length spiral wire.*
❀ *Copper wire 0.5mm, 9 cm long.*

METHOD

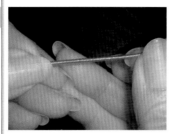

1. Gently stretch a length of spiral wire.

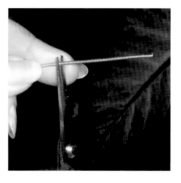

2. Cut a length of the stretched spiral wire 3.5 cm long.

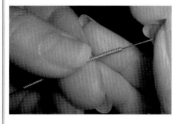

3. Pass a length of wire (0.5mm) 9cm. long through the piece of spiral wire.

4. Bend wire to form loop and using bent nose pliers, twist (0.5mm) wires together

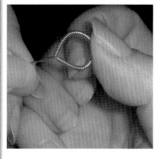

5. Gently shape petal

6. Make slip knot at base of frame. Take thread to top of petal and pass thread through the groove between the spirals

7. Take thread to bottom of petal and insert it in the first groove on the right hand side of the starting point. Take thread to the top left hand side.

8. Work spirographically, that is working from bottom right to top left until frame is filled. When complete make two turns at the base and finish off by making another slip knot.

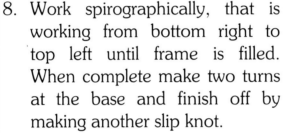

What we have completed is a round shaped petal, we can however make petals of different shapes and while the method of making the framework is the same, there could be slight variations when the frame work is being filled due to the shape of the frame and medium being used.

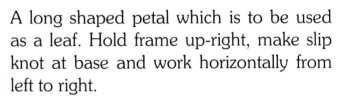

A long shaped petal which is to be used as a leaf. Hold frame up-right, make slip knot at base and work horizontally from left to right.

When top of petal is reached insert thread from back to front in the middle groove. Bring thread down to the base, stretch carefully to form rib, make two rounds and finish off by making a slip knot.

To make a long petal. Tie thread at base of petal. Take thread to top of petal and insert it in the third groove left of centre, take thread to right from back and work horizontally until the bottom is reached. Finish off by making two rounds and a slip knot.

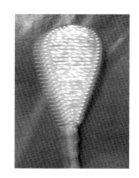

This is a round petal. To fill in the framework, follow the instructions in paragraphs 6,7 and 8 on page 70-71.

The triangular petal is in fact a round petal with the top part slightly flattened down. The framework is filled in exactly the same way as the round petal

The square petal. To make framework, pass a piece of 0.5mm wire through the spiral wire. Fold down the middle and bring the two halves side by side. Hold from top end and using tweezers, bend inwards the right hand half from the middle, likewise bend the left hand half. Bring ends of spiral wire next to each other and twist the 0.5mm wire together using bent nose pliers.

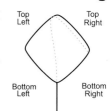

To fill frame work, make two rounds and a slip knot at the base of the frame.

Take thread from front to top corner and insert thread in the third groove of the top left side. Pass thread from back into opposite groove of the bottom right side. Take thread from front into the next groove of the bottom right side. Repeat process. filling all but the last two or three grooves, finishing off at top left corner.

Pass thread from back of petal to the third groove in top right side. Take thread directly opposite to the third groove in the upper corner of the bottom left side. Pass thread from back and insert once again in the next groove in top right side and again from the front to the next groove on bottom left side. Repeat process filling all but the last two or three grooves and finishing off in the lower corner of the bottom left side. Make two rounds on stem and secure with slip knot.

Three pointed petal. Make framework, and using tweezers make the three points. To fill framework, make two rounds and a slip knot at the base of frame. Take thread to top left of petal, insert in groove and working from back to front, fill frame. Make two rounds on stem and take thread between left and centre point. Make one round and bring thread down the front to base of petal. Make two rounds and once again take thread to top of petal between centre and right point, again make one round between points and bring thread down the front of petal. Finish off by making two rounds and secure with slip knot.

To make framework, pass a piece of 0.5mm wire through the spiral wire. Fold down the middle and bring the two halves side by side. Using pliers, twist the copper wires together. Gently separate the two halves from the middle, insert the ends of the bent nose pliers and carefully open the pliers until you get the desired shape. Holding frame from base in the left hand, take the top between forefinger and thumb and using slight pressure bend over forefinger.

To fill in the framework, follow the instructions in paragraphs 6, 7 and 8 on page 70-71.

Working with Spiral Wire

All the flowers on this page can be made using the given measurements and techniques described in Section 31.

MATERIALS

* *Four buds and leaves.*
* *Silver plated wire 0.25mm*
* *Copper wire 0.2mm*
* *Copper wire 0.5mm*
* *Sixteen pieces of stretched spiral wire (Molla) each 4.5cm long.*
* *Blue Rayon Floss (teased out to one ply).*
* *Prepared thread made with Green Rayon Floss and green wire.(0.25mm)*
* *16 glass beads*
* *Anima: 4 pieces, 1mm, 6cm long and 1 piece1.5mm. 10cm long*
* *Floral tape*

METHOD

Using the silver plated wire bead the 16 glass beads for stamens (4 stamens for each bud)

Using the stretched spiral wire and 0.5mm copper wire make 16 long petal frames and shape them using the technique described in the last paragraph of page 76. Fill framework horizontally with blue rayon floss, following instructions on page 74.

With green prepared thread make 9 leaves (Basic petal) each 1.9cm long starting with 9 rounds.

MOUNTING

Following the technique described in Section 4, page 9, under Second Method, mount leaves in groups of three.

To make bud, cover about 2cm of anima with floral tape. Bind stamens together by winding 0.2mm wire four or five rounds around stems. Do not cut binding wire. Place stamens against anima with beads just over the top and wind binding wire three or four times. Place first petal against anima just beneath the stamens and bind. Following this procedure, individually bind the remaining three petals. Wind the binding wire tightly all along petal stems making sure that rounds do not overlap. Cut

binding wire and cover with floral tape

Using the same method, mount the remaining buds. Place a group of three leaves against each bud, bind tightly together and cover with floral tape.

Cover the 1.5mm anima with floral tape, place bud with three groups of leaves against anima and bind tightly and cover with floral tape. In the same way bind the remaining buds to the anima, covering with floral tape when each bud is bound to the anima

Two Layered Flower

❋ *5 pieces stretched spiral wire, each 4.5cm long*
❋ *7 pieces stretched spiral wire, each 5 cm long.*
❋ *Ivory Rayon Floss (teased out to one ply).*
❋ *Red rhinestone*
❋ *Silver plated wire 0.25mm*
❋ *Copper wire 0.2mm*
❋ *Copper wire 0.5mm*
❋ *Anima 1mm, 6cm long*
❋ *Floral tape*

With rhinestone and silver plated wire 0.25mm make stamen. Using the stretched pieces of spiral wire, and 0.5 copper wire make 12 round petal frames following the technique described in pages 76 and 77.

Fill in the framework, using the ivory coloured thread and the instructions on page 79

Mount flower on 1mm anima, using instructions on page 21.

Square Petal Flower

❈ For 1 Flower:
❈ 5 pieces stretched gold spiral wire each 5cm long,
❈ Orange Rayon Floss (teased out to one ply)
❈ 5 red glass beads
❈ Gold plated wire 0.25mm
❈ Copper wire 0.2mm
❈ Copper wire 0.5mm
❈ Anima 1mm, 6cm long
❈ Floral tape

Using the stretched pieces of spiral wire, and 0.5 copper wire make 5 square petal frames following the technique described on page 79.

Fill in the framework, using the orange coloured thread and the instructions on page 79. Make sure that petals overlap.

Mount flower on 1mm anima.

Make and Create

Try making these beautiful flowers. By now you should have mastered the technique and you should have no difficulty in making the flowers shown on this page. Better still try experimenting with colours and the various petals and try to create new examples.

Part of the focal point of a garland adorning the tabernacle of our Lady of Ransom chapel at Selmun Malta

Ganutell

Ganutell, sometimes referred to as bouillon or elastic wire, gave this fascinating Maltese craft its name and it is only fitting that this last Section is devoted to flowers entirely or partly made of this versatile material.

Fancy Flower - Ganutell Teardrops

* *7 teardrops*
* *1 pearl*
* *Gold ganutell 2.5mm*
* *Gold wire 0.25 mm and 0.5mm*
* *Anima 1mm, 6cms long*
* *Copper wire 0.2mm*
* *Floral tape*

1. Cut a length of ganutell 2.5mm equal to the perimeter of the teardrop.
2. Pass 0.25mm gold wire through the ganutell.
3. Cut piece of 0.5mm wire 6 cms long for stem.
4. With the 0.25mm wire make two rounds on stem at about 1.5cm from the top,
5. Insert teardrop with narrow part facing downwards, take wire to top and make one round, take wire to bottom of teardrop and make another round,
6. Repeat process another time.
7. Slide ganutell along wire, to rest against base.
8. Encircle the teardrop with ganutell, passing the ganutell behind the protruding part of the stem and finish off by making two rounds at the base of the teardrop.
9. Bend protruding part at top of stem, embedding wire in ganutell to form a hook. This ensures that ganutell is firmly in place.

Repeat process for the remaining teardrops.

The next step is to decorate the pearl at centre of flower with ganutell.

1. Cut a piece of the same ganutell equal in length to the circumference of the pearl.
2. Cut a piece of 0.25 wire approximately 12cm long insert ganutell, placing it in the middle of the wire. Cross over wire and insert one of the ends through the ganutell and tighten to form a loop,
3. Hold loop in left hand with the two wires facing upwards and slip pearl in any one of the wires.
4. Bend wire with pearl downwards, at the same time placing pearl in loop and bending wire over the loop.
5. Bring wire down against the other and twist together.

MOUNTING

Cover about 2cm of anima and mount flower in the usual way.

Fancy Flower – Ganutell, Pearl, Beads and Basic Petals.

Maria Kerr

MATERIALS

❋ *Prepared thread any colour*
❋ *Silver ganutell 2mm*
❋ *8 pearls*
❋ *32 glass beads, same colour as thread*
❋ *5 glass beads for stamens, a shade darker than prepared thread*
❋ *Silver wire 0.25mm*
❋ *Copper wire 0.5 and 0.2mm*
❋ *Floral tape*
❋ *Anima 1mm, 6cm long*

METHOD

1. Make 5 basic petals 1.6cm starting with 5 rounds.
2. Measure length of 4 beads and a pearl and cut 8 pieces of ganutell equal to twice this length plus 0.5cm

3. Following technique used for making petals with spiral wire on Page 76 make 8 frames.

4. Insert 2 glass beads, a pearl and another 2 glass beads on a piece of 0.25 silver wire.

5. Shape frame as a long petal (See page 78),and Using the silver wire with inserted beads and pearl, make two rounds at base of frame. Slide beads and pearls against base and make one round on top of frame, pass wire through the beads and pearls finishing off by making two rounds on the bottom of the frame.

6. Repeat process to fill in remaining seven frames.

7. Bead the five glass beads on 0.25mm wire for stamens.

MOUNTING Cover about 2cm of anima with floral tape and mount flower in the usual way.

Ganutell Flower

The petals of this flower, although made out of Ganutell, are in fact basic petals

MATERIALS

❋ *Gold ganutell 2mm*
❋ *Gold wire 0.5mm and 0.25mm*
❋ *45 jade glass beads,*
❋ *1 gold glass bead*
❋ *Anima 1mm, 6cm long*
❋ *Floral tape*

METHOD

1. Cut a piece of 0.5mm wire, 6cm long
2. Cut a piece of ganutell 10 cm long.
3. Cut a piece of gold wire 0.25mm, 15 cm long.

4. Insert 0.25mm wire through ganutell.

5. Make 2 rounds at about 2.5cm from top of 0.5mm wire, with the 0.25 wire protruding through ganutell.

6. Slide three glass beads into the 0.5mm wire and bring them to rest on the two rounds. Slide ganutell to rest underneath the glass beads, using the ganutell covered wire instead of prepared thread, work a basic petal using the technique described in Section 3 - The Basic Petal.

7. Make another four petals to complete the first   layer.

8. Repeat paragraphs 4 to 7 to make a basic petal.

9. Make a further six petals to complete the second layer.

10. With the remaining beads make cluster for centre of flower. (See Stamen 4 on page 15)

Tulips and Daffodils

❋ *Prepared thread made of yellow Rayon Floss and gold wire 0.25mm*
❋ *Copper wire 0.5 and 0.2mm*
❋ *5 pieces anima 1mm*
❋ *Glass beads*
❋ *Floral tape*

METHOD

10 square petals 2cm

30 basic petals 2.2cm starting with 11 rounds

6 beaded glass beads for each daffodil

MATERIALS (TULIPS)

❋ *Prepared thread made with a darker shade of yellow and gold wire .25mm*
❋ *Copper wire 0.5 and 0.2mm*
❋ *5 pieces anima 1mm*
❋ *Glass beads*
❋ *Floral tape*

METHOD

36 basic petals 2.5cm starting with 10 rounds

6 beaded glass beads for each tulip

MATERIALS

❋ *One layered flowers*
❋ *Prepared thread made with white rayon floss and silver wire 0.25mm*
❋ *Copper wire 0.5 and 0.2mm*
❋ *5 pieces copper wire*

33 Project

Tulips And Daffodils

METHOD

MATERIALS

METHOD

✤ Glass beads
✤ Floral tape

15 basic petals 1.6cm starting with 5 rounds

10 basic petals 1.8 starting with 6 rounds

✤ Leaves
✤ Green rayon floss and green wire 0.25mm

25 leaves, each leaf 1.9cm starting with 9 rounds

5 long leaves